Who On Earth is Jane Goodall?

Champion for the Chimpanzees

Read about other Scientists
Saving the Earth

Who on Earth is Aldo Leopold?
Father of Wildlife Ecology
ISBN: 978-1-59845-115-3
ISBN: 1-59845-115-4

Who on Earth is Archie Carr?
Protector of Sea Turtles
ISBN: 978-1-59845-120-7
ISBN: 1-59845-120-0

Who on Earth is Dian Fossey?
Defender of the Mountain Gorillas
ISBN: 978-1-59845-117-7
ISBN: 1-59845-117-0

Who on Earth is Jane Goodall?
Champion for the Chimpanzees
ISBN: 978-1-59845-119-1
ISBN: 1-59845-119-7

Who on Earth is Rachel Carson?
Mother of the Environmental Movement
ISBN: 978-1-59845-116-0
ISBN: 1-59845-116-2

Scientists Saving the Earth

Who On Earth is Jane Goodall?

Champion for the Chimpanzees

Victoria Guidi

Enslow Publishers, Inc.
40 Industrial Road
Box 398
Berkeley Heights, NJ 07922
USA

http://www.enslow.com

Library of Congress Cataloging-in-Publication Data

Guidi, Victoria.
  Who on earth is Jane Goodall? : champion for the chimpanzees / Victoria Guidi.
      p. cm. — (Scientists saving the earth)
  Includes bibliographical references and index.
  Summary: "Details Jane Goodall's life, with chapters devoted to her early years, life, work,
writings, and foundations"—Provided by publisher.
  ISBN-13: 978-1-59845-119-1
  ISBN-10: 1-59845-119-7
  1. Goodall, Jane, 1934 – —Juvenile literature. 2. Primatologists—England—Biography—Juvenile
literature. 3. Women primatologists—England—Biography—Juvenile literature. 4. Chimpanzees—
Tanzania—Gombe Stream National Park—Juvenile literature. I. Title.
  QL31.G58G85 2009
  590.92—dc22
  [B]

                                        2008032015

Printed in the United States of America
102010 Lake Book Manufacturing, Inc., Melrose Park, IL

10 9 8 7 6 5 4 3 2

To Our Readers:
We have done our best to make sure all Internet Addresses in this book were active and appropriate
when we went to press. However, the author and the publisher have no control over and assume no
liability for the material available on those Internet sites or on other Web sites they may link to. Any
comments or suggestions can be sent by e-mail to comments@enslow.com or to the address on the
back cover.

♲ Enslow Publishers, Inc., is committed to printing our books on recycled paper. The paper in every
book contains 10% to 30% post-consumer waste (PCW). The cover board on the outside of each book
contains 100% PCW. Our goal is to do our part to help young people and the environment too!

Photo Credits: Andrew Cohen, University of Arizona at Tucson; National Science Foundation;
p. 31; © Associated Press, pp. 80, 84, © Baron Hugo Van Lawick/National Geographic Image
Collection, pp. 36, 53, 59, 63; U.S. Department of Defense, p. 22; © Donnchadh Kennedy, pp. 6, 98;
© Durova, p. 27(bottom); © Enslow Publishers, Inc., pp. 19, 29; © Gerry Ellis/Getty Images,
pp. 42(bottom); © Getty Images, pp. 38, 40, 46; Library of Congress, p. 20; © Newell-Smith/Globe
Photos, p. 33; © Photo by Curt Busse, pp. 9, 45, 71, 74; © Shutterstock, p. 17; © smartneddy, p. 42
(top); U.S. Department of the Interior/Bureau of Land Management, p. 27 (top); Wikimedia, pp. 13,
93.

Cover Photo: Jane Goodall observes (from left) Tess, 5 or 6 years old, Sophie, 7, and Bahati, 3,
eating at the Sweetwaters Chimpanzee Sanctuary near Nanyuki (north of Nairobi) on Sunday,
December 6, 1997. Credit: Associated Press

Contents

1

Jane Goodall observing chimps at Gombe.

The Rain Dance of the Chimpanzees

Twenty-six-year-old Jane Goodall had started the morning watching a large group of chimpanzees. They were about one hundred yards down a grassy slope that was scattered with trees. Several young chimps were immersed in a game of tag. They played wildly in the trees, chasing one another, wrestling, swinging from branch to branch. In sight, then out of sight. It was hard to keep a steady focus on the frisky bunch.

Goodall redirected her attention to a smaller group feeding in the trees. There were five adult males and one female. Soon, the adults climbed from their trees into a single tree. Just as they made themselves comfortable, the young chimps reappeared, ending the peace and quiet.

Then came the rain. Large droplets of water landed on Goodall as she sat waiting to see what the chimpanzees would do. The rain came down harder. Thunder shook the sky.

Finally, Paleface made a move. He climbed down and sat hunched in the grass under a tree. He stared directly at Goodall. Soon, another adult male sat near him.

Jane Goodall looked on motionless as the rest of the apes in the tree quietly made their way down. They formed two groups. In parallel lines, they began to saunter up the slope in the pelting rain. The apes moved in single file. Goodall could not believe how organized it all was.

Lightning flashed as the marchers neared the top of the hillside. Paleface broke into a run. He swiped at a bush with his hand and charged down the slope. He tore off a branch that hung above him. He waved it like a wand until he reached a tree at the bottom, spun around, and climbed back up to the top. One by one, the other males charged down the slope. The other chimpanzees took seats in the branches and watched as the

⊙These chimps exemplified the displays of aggression that Jane Goodall described.

males danced to the sound track of rolling thunder and blazing lightning.

In a half hour, the dance was over. The male performers climbed into the trees and glanced at the one human in their audience.

Was it for me? Goodall wondered.

The chimpanzees silently started up the slope. Jane Goodall wrote in her journal: "Paleface was the last to go. He stood up, holding a sapling in his left hand, looking back at me. His giant silhouette against the grey sky was impressive. Awe inspiring. The actor taking his curtain call."[1]

It was January 31, 1961, and twenty-six-year-old Jane Goodall was at Gombe Stream Reserve in Tanzania, Africa. She had been sent there a few months earlier with an assignment: to study the behavior of chimpanzees in the wild.

Every day, Goodall ventured out into the forests in search of the wild chimpanzees. Every time she came onto the scene, no matter how far away she was, they hurried off into the forest. Now, after the rain dance it seemed the wild chimpanzees were beginning to acknowledge her.

One day, she heard a group of chimpanzees approaching from behind. She lay down in the grass so they would not see her and run away. The group settled by a tree that was full of fruit and began to eat.

She heard footsteps. Then they stopped. A worried call alerted Goodall that she had been spotted.

A large male chimpanzee climbed into a tree just next to where she lay. He made his way out on the branches that hung over her. He shook the branches wildly and screamed. Then he descended the tree and stood close enough for Goodall to see his yellow teeth and pink tongue. After a few more displays of aggression, he disappeared.

Goodall looked around and saw a female with her baby staring at her from another tree. Again, footsteps approached from behind. They came straight up to Jane and stopped.

Wham! Something powerful hit her head. She sat up. Right in front of her stood the male. He stared at her, and Goodall thought for certain that he was going to charge. Instead, he turned and started walking off. Every so often he stopped to turn back and stare at Goodall.

Quietly, the female chimp and her child climbed down from the tree and followed the male.

What was she thinking? Clearly, the chimpanzee's fear had turned into aggression that now proved physically dangerous. Jane Goodall was young and had her whole life ahead of her. Why risk it like this?

Even if her life was at risk, however, Jane Goodall had no intention of leaving anytime soon.

2

A Curious Child

Valerie Jane Goodall was born on April 3, 1934, in London, England. Her baby sister, Judith Daphne, came four years later. Her father, Mortimer Goodall, was an engineer and a successful race car driver. Her mother, Margaret Myfanwe Joseph, or Vanne as she was called, had gone to secretarial school and was working as a secretary when she and Mortimer met. The two married in 1932. Vanne soon quit her secretarial job to become a full-time housewife, mother, and supporter of her husband's career.

Jane Goodall is pictured with her stuffed-animal chimpanzee which accompanies her during her travels.

A Perfect Match

Mortimer may very well have been the light that sparked Valerie Jane's love for chimpanzees. As the story goes, one day Mortimer was searching for a present for Valerie Jane's first birthday. He saw a stuffed toy chimpanzee in the window of a toy shop. The chimpanzee had been produced as a token of celebration for the arrival of the London Zoo's first captive-born chimpanzee, Jubilee. Mortimer thought it was the perfect cuddly toy for a one-year-old. Certain family members and friends did not think it was the perfect gift for a young child.

However, Jubilee proved to be the ideal companion. To Goodall, he "was my most loved possession and accompanied me on all my childhood travels."[1]

Around the same time Valerie Jane received Jubilee, the Goodall family moved to the suburbs outside of London. They lived on a quiet street where Valerie Jane was able to explore the outside world.

Once, after playing in the yard, Jane took a handful of earthworms to bed with her. She buried some under her pillow. They were soon discovered by her nanny who wanted Valerie Jane to be reprimanded for such behavior. Vanne did not believe that what Valerie Jane did was wrong. She said to the curious child, "Well, Valerie Jane, if you keep these wormes [sic] there all night, they'll be dead in the morning. They really ought to go into the garden where they belong."[2] Valerie Jane understood and scooped up the earthworms and put them back in the earth.

Another time, while at a family friend's beach house, Valerie Jane took a bunch of seashells back to her room. Soon little sea snails were crawling everywhere. Her mother explained that the snails' home was the sea and without it they would die. So Valerie Jane made a mad dash to gather all the sea snails and hurry them back to the sea.[3]

Change

In May 1939, Mortimer moved the family to France to devote himself to racing full-time. Near the end of that first summer, the family was advised to get out of the country as quickly as possible. German leader Adolf Hitler had invaded its eastern neighboring country, Czechoslovakia. France shared Germany's western border. It was not safe to remain in France. The family moved back to England. They stayed at the Manor House where Mortimer's mother and siblings lived. On September 3, 1939, Neville Chamberlain, prime minister of England, declared war on Germany. World War II had begun.

Missing!

One afternoon, Vanne had gone for the day to volunteer for the war effort. When she returned to the Manor House, she went looking for Valerie Jane. The young child was nowhere around the house. Panic quickly set in. Minutes turned into hours as the search for Valerie Jane continued. The police were called.

Suddenly, Valerie Jane emerged from across the field by the henhouses. When asked where she had been, her answer, "with a hen," must have bewildered everyone.

Vanne said, "But you've been away for nearly five hours. What can you possibly have been doing with a hen all that time?"

Valerie Jane replied, "I had to find out how hens lay eggs, so I went into a hen coop to find out. . . . It was a long time, but [a hen] came at last, and then she laid an egg. . . . Suddenly she gave a little wiggle and—plop!—it landed on the straw."[4] At the age of five, Jane had carried out her first research project.

Around this same time, Goodall's father enlisted with the British army to help fight in the war. He was assigned to posts overseas. Vanne took her daughters to live at her mother's house in Bournemouth, England.

Bournemouth Town, Lower Gardens. Jane and her mother moved to Bournemouth when she was 12 years old.

A Place to Call Home

Bournemouth is a small beach town that lies on the south coast of England. Vanne's mother and two sisters lived at the estate.

It seemed the perfect place for Valerie Jane's love of nature to grow. It had a big garden, lots of green grass, and many trees to climb. There were lots of earth's creatures to discover, too. Only this time around, V.J.—Valerie Jane's nickname—did not always leave the critters and crawlers where they belonged.

V.J. started her own menagerie. There were caterpillars, racing snails, Hamlett the hamster, and Peter the canary. There were the guinea pigs: Ghandi, Jimmy, and Spindle. (Unfortunately, Spindle's life was short-lived as a result of Pickles the cat.) V.J. took great care of her collection. She made sure each animal was regularly fed, cleaned, and exercised. She loved her animals.

The Gift of Reading

V.J. was fascinated by Hugh Lofting's Doctor Doolittle books. She wanted to be just like the character Dr. Doolittle—the veterinarian who was friends with all the animals. His house was full of them. "Besides the gold-fish in the pond at the bottom of his garden, he had rabbits in the pantry, white mice in his piano, a squirrel in the linen closet and a hedgehog in the cellar. . . ."[5]

V.J. received her first Dr. Doolittle book for Christmas in 1942. In *The Story of Dr. Doolittle,* Dr. Doolittle is taught by his pet parrot, Polynesia, to speak the language of animals. Now the animal doctor would be able to talk to all the animals that were sick. Instead of him having to guess what the problem was, the animals would simply tell Dr. Doolittle their symptoms, and he would know what was wrong with them.

In one of the book's chapters, Chee Chee, the monkey, cries, "I've just had a message from a cousin of mine

THE FAREWELL FEAST

"After they had all finished eating the Doctor got up"

Illustration from *Dr. Doolittle.*

in Africa. There is a terrible sickness among the monkeys out there. They are all catching it—and they are dying in hundreds. They . . . beg you to come to Africa to stop the sickness."[6]

Dr. Doolittle and some of his animals piled into a boat to go to Africa. After many weeks in rough seas and in the forests of Africa, the doctor finally reached the monkeys and was able to save them.

Yet, it was Tarzan of the Apes who the blonde-haired girl really loved. Every time V.J. opened Edgar Rice Burroughs' *Tarzan of the Jungle* she fell in love all over again. Tarzan, the lost son of English parents, was raised by a female ape in the jungle. Then he rescued a woman named Jane and the two fell in love. "I was incredibly jealous of Tarzan's Jane and I thought she was a real wimp, and I'd have made a much better mate for Tarzan myself," Goodall said in an interview. "That was when I had this dream of going to Africa."[7]

At eight years old, V.J. made up her mind that she would go to Africa to

Tarzan movie poster.

live with the wild animals, speak to them, study them, and write about them.

Childhood in a Time of War

Growing up in Europe during World War II was not easy. The rumble of distant bombs and the constant roar of plane engines overhead were nonstop. Food and other goods had to be rationed. Goodall recalled of the time, "Although my own life was still filled with love and security, I was slowly becoming aware of another kind of world altogether, a harsh and bitter world of pain and death and human cruelty."[8] It was a horrific and nightmarish war that brought twenty-five million people to their deaths, including Goodall's beloved uncle.

Although V.J.'s family did not have a lot of money, they had what mattered. They had support and values. Goodall had a mother who encouraged her to follow her dreams. "Jane, if you really want something, and if you work hard, take advantage of the opportunities, and never give up, you will somehow find a way."[9] Vanne was an important role model to her daughter.

Mortimer, V.J.'s father, seemed to disappear into the war effort. His letters arrived less frequently as World War II waged on. Mortimer and Vanne finally divorced in 1950.

The war officially ended on May 7, 1945. Photographs of the Nazi death camps splashed the pages of newspapers. Goodall struggled to make sense of it all. "All the evil aspects of human nature had been given free rein, all the values I had been taught—the values of kindness and decency and love—had been disregarded. . . . [H]ow could human beings do such unspeakable things to other human beings?"[10]

Building Skills

Around 1945, Goodall began horseback-riding lessons. She also took on a new nickname, Spindle. Spindle learned a lot about handling large animals.

These survivors of a Nazi death camp were found nearly starved to death. Here, they are being taken to a hospital for medical attention.

She learned from their behaviors what the horses were trying to communicate. She started to understand their language.

Spindle also learned a lot from her pet dog, Rusty. Their time together taught Spindle an incredible amount about the true nature of animals.

In the summer of 1946, Spindle started the Alligator Club with some neighborhood friends. It was a nature club. Spindle, now Red Admiral (self-assigned), was its leader. She led the club members on guided nature tours and even held a fund-raiser for old horses. She published the *Alligator Letter*, a magazine with puzzles, quizzes, nature notes, and articles on subjects like birds' eggs and animal tracks.

Teenage Life

There was growing up to do. Gradually, she abandoned the nicknames V.J., Spindle, and Red Admiral, and settled simply for Jane.

Jane did very well in school, particularly in English, history, and biology. At home, she read philosophy books. She continued to write, and even won first prize for a writing contest at school.

One Man's Sermon

One Sunday, Jane attended a church service with her grandmother. The reverend's message was powerful but expressed in a very simple way. Jane decided she was going to start attending church regularly.

Church became a very important part of Jane's teenage life. She enjoyed reading the Bible and its many wonderful stories. It read like poetry to her.

Childhood's End

Jane was a dreamer, but her dream seemed so far away. She wanted to be a zoologist and study the behavior of wild animals in Africa. However, in 1952, career choices for women were limited to being a teacher, nurse, or secretary. Jobs in zoology were strictly for men.

Jane graduated from high school in 1952. If her family could have afforded it, she would have gone to a university. Instead, she took her savings and spent three months in Germany. When she returned, she began secretarial school in London. Secretarial skills were skills she knew she could use anywhere around the world. She then began to work at a film production company.

A few years passed until one day in 1956, when Jane received a letter from Clo, a childhood friend. Clo had moved to the country of Kenya with her family, and there was an invitation for Jane to come and stay with them in Africa.

3

Off to Africa

Jane Goodall would have bought her ticket that same day she received Clo's invitation to Kenya. Unfortunately, her bank account was empty. Straightaway, she quit her job at the film company, left London, and returned to Bournemouth to waitress and save some money.

Two and a half months later, she boarded the steamship *Kenya Castle*. The boat reached southern Africa on April 2, 1957. A day later, she was in Nairobi, the capital of Kenya. Jane Goodall was twenty-three years old.

After little more than a month in Nairobi, Goodall began work as a typist for a British-owned construction company.

First Impressions Make the Difference

"If you are interested in animals, you must see Louis Leakey," someone told her one day.[1] Louis Leakey was a very important and well-known archaeologist and paleontologist. A paleontologist studies the fossils of animals and plants. Leakey was also the curator of the Cordyndon Museum, Nairobi's natural history museum.

Goodall made an appointment with Leakey. "From the moment we met he enchanted me with his knowledge of Africa and its people and animals. Fortunately I apparently enchanted him too with my youthful enthusiasm, my love of animals, and my determination to get to Africa. . . . I think [also] he was impressed that someone with no degree understood the meaning of words like *ichthyology* and *herpetology*."[2] Ichthyology is a branch of zoology that deals with fishes. Herpetology is a branch of zoology dealing with reptiles and amphibians.

The two spent hours together touring the museum. Leakey knew there was something unique about this young Englishwoman. At the end of their meeting, Leakey asked Goodall to be his secretary beginning that September. His previous secretary had left to study gorillas. Goodall accepted.

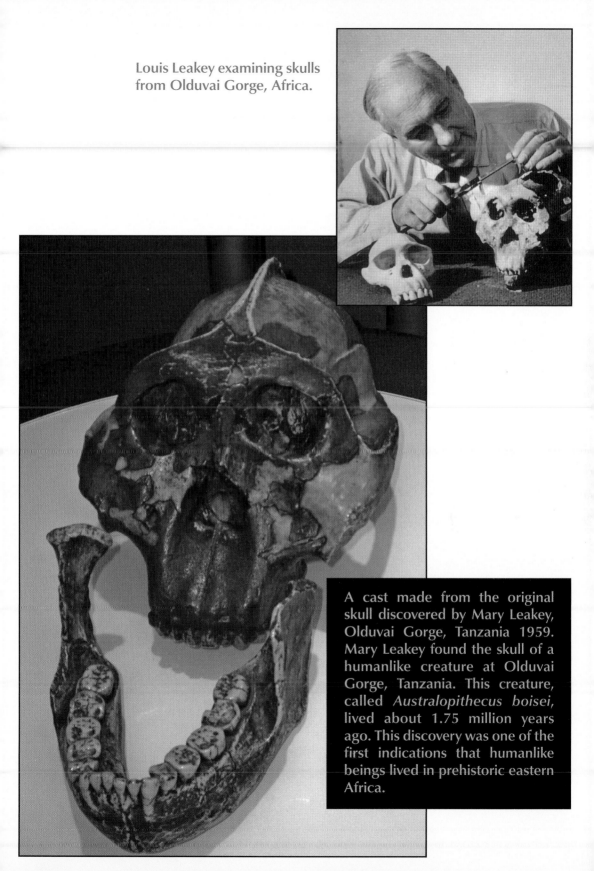

Louis Leakey examining skulls from Olduvai Gorge, Africa.

A cast made from the original skull discovered by Mary Leakey, Olduvai Gorge, Tanzania 1959. Mary Leakey found the skull of a humanlike creature at Olduvai Gorge, Tanzania. This creature, called *Australopithecus boisei*, lived about 1.75 million years ago. This discovery was one of the first indications that humanlike beings lived in prehistoric eastern Africa.

Digging Up Life's Past

Soon after, Leakey came to Goodall with another proposal. Leakey and his wife ran an archeological expedition to Olduvai Gorge in Tanganyika every year. The couple went to look for fossils. They found a lot of simple stone tools, but not any remains of the apelike humans who had made and used them. Leakey asked Goodall if she would like to join them in this search. Again, Goodall accepted.

One evening, Leakey told Goodall about an idea that he had had for a long time. It had to do with the African great apes: chimpanzees, bonobos, and gorillas. Leakey wanted to sponsor a long-term study of them. But this study would not be like any other one. What he had in mind was something entirely new to the field.

Leakey studied fossils and ancient human bones. Bones can be pieced back together to help create pictures of what life looked like thousands of years ago. But skeletons and remains from ancient times cannot tell us much about how our ancestors behaved. Leakey thought about studying apes in the wild. This species is the closest living relative to humans. Their genetic material, or DNA, is almost identical to that of humans. Understanding the behavior of these animals in their natural habitat, Leakey believed, would help us understand how our Stone Age ancestors may

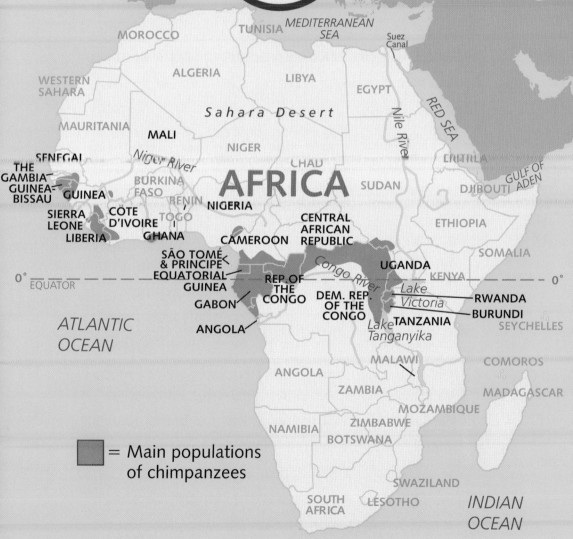

Chimpanzee Range Map

MOROCCO
TUNISIA
MEDITERRANEAN SEA
Suez Canal

WESTERN SAHARA
ALGERIA
LIBYA
EGYPT

MAURITANIA
Sahara Desert
MALI
NIGER
CHAD
SUDAN
RED SEA
ERITREA
GULF OF ADEN
DJIBOUTI

SENEGAL
Niger River
BURKINA FASO
AFRICA

THE GAMBIA
GUINEA-BISSAU
GUINEA
BENIN
TOGO
NIGERIA
CENTRAL AFRICAN REPUBLIC
ETHIOPIA

SIERRA LEONE
CÔTE D'IVOIRE
GHANA
CAMEROON
SOMALIA

LIBERIA
SÃO TOMÉ & PRINCIPE
EQUATORIAL GUINEA
Congo River
UGANDA
KENYA

0°
EQUATOR
REP. OF THE CONGO
DEM. REP. OF THE CONGO
Lake Victoria
RWANDA
0°

GABON
BURUNDI

ATLANTIC OCEAN
ANGOLA
TANZANIA
SEYCHELLES

Lake Tanganyika
MALAWI
COMOROS

ANGOLA
ZAMBIA
MOZAMBIQUE
MADAGASCAR

NAMIBIA
ZIMBABWE
BOTSWANA

■ = Main populations of chimpanzees

SWAZILAND

SOUTH AFRICA
LESOTHO
INDIAN OCEAN

have behaved. Leaky also believed that a study of this kind would give people insight into the evolutionary past of humans.

Me? Study the Chimps?

After the expedition ended, Goodall continued her work at the museum. Leakey continued to bring up his ape study idea. Finally, Goodall said, "Louis, I wish you wouldn't keep talking about it because that's just what I want to do." Leakey replied, "Jane, I've been waiting for you to tell me that. Why on earth did you think I talked about those chimpanzees to you?"[3]

Jane Goodall could not believe the next words she heard. Leakey asked if she would be interested in studying the chimpanzees. But with no formal education? No scientific background? No prior experience? No credentials? And as a woman?

Leakey was 100 percent sure of his pick. In fact, he wanted someone "with a mind uncluttered and unbiased by theory who would make the study for no other reason that a real desire for knowledge."[4] He believed a woman would prove better than a man at studying animal behavior. A woman would be more patient and appear less threatening.

The place for the study was already chosen. It would be at Gombe Stream Chimpanzee Reserve in the Tanganyika Territory. That territory is now the country of Tanzania. The species lived in an area just off Lake Tanganyika.

Goodall would later recall: "I could have gone on at the museum. Or I could have learned a whole lot more about fossils and become a paleontologist. But both these careers had to do with dead animals. And I still wanted to work with living animals. My childhood dream was as strong as ever: . . . I wanted to come as close to talking to animals as I could."[5]

Jane Goodall's decision: yes.

Yes Is Easy, Now the Difficult Part

It was very difficult raising money for the study. Many people doubted that it would be a success. Who could take it seriously after hearing that a

Lake Tanganyika in Africa, near the Gombe Stream Chimpanzee Reserve.

twenty-three-year-old unqualified secretary would be doing it?

There was no way that the British government would allow any European woman into the Gombe Stream Chimpanzee Reserve by herself. To live with wild chimpanzees was not only a crazy idea but a very dangerous one. Only if a suitable European companion went with Goodall would they allow the study to happen. Vanne immediately agreed to be her daughter's escort.

On February 12, 1959, Leakey received money from the Wilkie Foundation for a four-month study. Goodall continued to work at the Naorobi museum. Then she returned to England and worked for a documentary film company at the London Zoo until the real adventure began.

The Adventure Begins

In July 1960, Goodall and Vanne headed for Gombe Stream Chimpanzee Reserve along an 840-mile-long road. When they reached the small town of Kigoma on Lake Tanganyika, they traveled another 16 miles up the lake to the reserve.

Gombe is filled with thick forests, deep valleys, and steep hills. When Goodall arrived, about 160 chimpanzees resided in the area. There were also buffalo, leopards, bushpigs, hippos, lizards, frogs, tortoises, and geckos. Insects such as termites, grasshoppers, and beetles scurried across the ground. Not to mention, a ton of mosquitoes all day, every day.

On July 14, 1960, Goodall, Vanne, Dominic, their African cook, and his wife, arrived at the village of Kasekela. They were showed to a clearing called Kakombe. This would serve as their campsite. Goodall and her team set up camp. Goodall and Vanne shared one tent, and Dominic and his wife shared another.

First Days of Exploring

A couple of days later, Goodall officially began her field study of the chimpanzees.

There were reports of a chimp spotting at a big *msulula* tree nearby. Goodall and her escorts chose a clearing near the tree and waited. Suddenly came the sounds of chimpanzees.

As a young single woman, Jane Goodall was not permitted by British officials to go into the African jungle by herself to study animals. She would have to choose a companion.

[A] chimpanzee climbed up a palm trunk and into the branches of the giant tree. It was followed by another and another and another, each climbing in orderly procession. I counted sixteen in all. . . . And then, one after the other and in complete silence the whole group climbed down the palm tree ladder and vanished into the forest . . . sixteen chimpanzees in one tree and yet the only sounds I had heard had been the calls announcing their arrival.[6]

For the next eight weeks, Goodall explored all over the reserve. She continued to see many chimpanzees eating red-and-yellow berries from *msulula* trees, but she was barely able to get within five hundred feet of them. Those weeks were very discouraging for Goodall. For so long she dreamed of this moment, when the animals of the wild would let her into their world.

Doctor Vanne

Vanne also found herself busy. Louis Leakey had made sure to send the women with enough first-aid supplies and medicine to treat a large community. He believed the best way to develop friendly relations with the local Africans was to give them medicine. Many Africans, however, did not trust Goodall and Vanne. They were suspicious of these two strange white women who had come to live in the jungle and watch chimpanzees.

The game ranger who took Goodall and Vanne to Gombe Stream told local Africans that the women would be more than happy to treat them for small illnesses. Vanne opened up a small clinic. By the second day, thirty people arrived. A week later there were sixty patients.[7]

Even Doctors Get Sick

About eight weeks into the study, both Goodall and Vanne contracted malaria, a disease that is passed on to humans by the bite of a mosquito. It is common in tropical regions. For nearly two weeks, both mother and daughter lay side by side in their tent with high fevers. They had barely enough strength to even speak.

Jane Goodall was already frustrated. She had been watching chimpanzees for three months. The animals would not allow her to get anywhere close to them. As soon as they spotted her, they fled. How long would it take for them to stop fearing her? She had other worries, too. "Would I succeed in learning anything really significant before the funding ran out? I knew perfectly well that if results didn't come through, Louis wouldn't be able to raise further money. I was terrified of letting him down."[8]

And on top of it all, now to be terribly ill and bedridden.

Back to Health, and Up to the Peak

As soon as her fever had gone down and she was feeling well enough, Goodall eagerly went back to

A small clearing, shaded by tall oil nut palms, became the campsite for Jane Goodall and her mother. Shown here are Jane and a local fisherman.

work. One morning, while it was still cool, she ventured out without telling anybody. She headed up a steep slope about forty-five minutes from camp. Finally, she reached a peak about halfway up. The clearing overlooked two valleys and open grassy ridges and slopes.

After about fifteen minutes, Goodall saw out of the corner of her eye something move. She turned around and saw three chimps staring at her from barely eight yards away. They stayed for a moment to gaze at the strange creature before calmly proceeding on their way into the thick vegetation. Soon another group came to feed on a fig tree. Then another group appeared. They all turned and stared at Goodall. The group quickened their pace, but did not run away in fear. Instead, they joined the group that was feeding. When all of the chimpanzees were satisfied, they got up and left.

Goodall returned to camp that evening very excited. The peak she had discovered turned out to be the ideal place to watch the chimpanzees from a long distance. It immediately became known as the Peak. Every morning for about a month, Goodall started her day on the Peak. And every day, chimpanzees ate from the fig trees below. As Goodall would later write, discovering the Peak "marked the turning point in my study. . . . Piece by piece, I began to form my first somewhat crude picture of chimpanzee life."[9]

Chimpanzees, so like us and yet so different, have long captured our imagination.

Beginning the Time of Discoveries

Goodall soon fell into a daily rhythm. Every morning, the alarm clock would wake her at 5:30. She would eat a slice of bread, make coffee, and then climb to the Peak while it was still dark out. Her vantage point from the Peak was very good, and she was able to catch some great observations about chimpanzee social behavior.

Goodall copiously recorded everything she could about the chimpanzees. She wrote down everything about their physical appearance and mannerisms. She tried to identify the different sounds they made throughout the day. She collected samples of what they ate. She watched them at bedtime.

To get closer to the chimpanzees, Goodall would mimic their actions. She made quiet grunting, panting sounds. She crawled about very slowly, with her hands made into fists. She scraped at tree bark and poked into the ground with sticks. She pulled down branches and nibbled on leaves. She avoided eye contact, but did not avoid being seen. If Goodall acted more like a chimpanzee, maybe she would not be seen as such a threat.

The Naming Game

Gradually, the chimpanzees of Gombe Center became less and less afraid of this strange-looking

Chimpanzees, like humans, are able to express a great deal with their faces.

"white ape." After about six months on the Peak, Goodall was able to recognize some chimpanzees. Mr. McGregor was one of the chimps easiest to recognize. He was named after the character of the old gardener from the book *Peter Rabbit*. He was old and almost completely bald from the shoulders up, except for a small spiky tuft of hair on the back of his head. Flo was also very easy to recognize. Her fat, bulging nose and ragged ears were easy to point out. Plus, her two sons, Figan and Faben, and daughter Fifi, were always with her.

There were William and Olly, who Goodall was convinced were brother and sister. And then there were David Greybeard and Goliath. "As I got to know them as individuals I named them. I had no idea that this, according to the ethological discipline of the early 1960s, was inappropriate—I should have given them more objective numbers."[10]

Many scientists during this time felt that study animals should be identified by numbers. To name them was anthropomorphic, or giving the animals human characteristics. By using numbers to identify them, any potential emotional attachment would be avoided.

Goodall was also committing another big no-no. When she wrote about the chimpanzees, she described their personalities. ". . . [I]n those days it was held (at least by many scientists, philosophers, and theologians) that only humans had minds,

George Schaller described his first silverback as the "most magnificent animal" he had ever seen. This mountain gorilla sports the characteristic silver-streaked hair of the mature male.

only humans were capable of rational thought."[11] Yet, "as I got to know them and watched them interact, their personalities became very obvious. There were mean ones and generous ones, aggressive ones and gentle ones."[12]

When Goodall found out she was being criticized for her methods of observation, she felt it didn't make sense. She thought about her own pets, who had not only names, but distinct personalities. These methods made complete sense to Goodall and she was not going to change her ways if she believed they were right.

Schaller's Words

In the meantime, Dr. Leakey got in touch with an important zoologist named George Schaller. Since February 1959, Schaller had been studying the mountain gorillas in East Africa. Leakey knew Schaller could advise Goodall on her work.

Schaller arrived at Gombe on October 8, 1960. He spent two days with Goodall. With the Gombe study coming to an end soon, what did Goodall have to show for her work? What significant findings did she have that would bring in more funding?

During one of their conversations, Schaller said, "If you see tool using and hunting [for meat], it will have made the whole study worthwhile."[13]

Little did Goodall know that someone, or something, besides her was listening to these words.

4

First Important Discovery

On Sunday, October 30, 1960, Jane Goodall started her morning off on the Peak. Just before 8:00 AM, she spotted a skirmish in the trees below. There were three chimpanzees. One held something pink in its hand. A fourth chimpanzee and a few baboons were nearby. The scene looked like a fight. After more than an hour of chasing and screaming, Goodall was able to see what the mysterious object was. It was bushpig meat.

Chimpanzees were not supposed to be meat eaters. Occasionally they ate small insects, but mainly they lived on fruits, nuts, and vegetables. This discovery was very significant to Goodall's study.

Louis Leakey had sent her on this study because he believed that humans and chimpanzees shared a common ancestor. Now, confirming that chimpanzees ate meat would bring him one great step closer to proving his theory.

I've Gone Fishing

The Friday following the meat-eating episode, Goodall made a second important discovery. "For a long time there has been heated discussion in

⟲ Chimp eating meat.

The ability to use objects, such as sticks, as tools sets chimpanzees and other apes apart from most other members of the animal kingdom.

scientific circles as to whether any primates in the wild ever modify natural objects to make tools. My chimpanzees have settled the argument once and for all: The answer is that at least some chimpanzees do."[1]

The civilized world believed that tool using and toolmaking were exclusively human acts. Yet, five days after the meat sighting, Goodall threw another curve ball at a popular belief.

It was November 4 when Goodall sat watching an adult male chimp squatting in front of a termite mound. She looked on as he picked up a blade of grass and poked it into the termite hole. Carefully, he pulled it out. Termites clung to the grass. Contently, he plucked off the termites and popped them into his mouth. The chimpanzee was "fishing" for termites with a tool that he had made himself.

As Goodall saw it, the act not only showed craft, but also reasoning and problem-solving skills. She sent a telegram to Leakey. He replied, "Now we must redefine 'tool,' redefine 'man,' or accept chimpanzees as humans."[2] It seemed that the link between chimpanzees and humans was getting closer and closer.

A University Degree and Scientific Conferences

The meat sighting and toolmaking discoveries meant two things to Leakey. The study was scheduled to end on December 1, 1960. If he was to keep his young aspiring female scientist on board he had to make some important moves. First, Goodall would need a university degree. Leakey said to her, "Jane you must have a Ph.D. because if you don't, you'll never be able to get your own money and stand on your own feet, nor will you be able to make use of your facts."' [3] Second, he would have to look for more funding so that the study would continue.

Goodall was accepted into the doctoral program in ethology at Cambridge University in England, despite her lack of any undergraduate education or degree. The National Geographic Society also gave her a grant of $1,400 to continue her study at Gombe.

In the winter of 1961, Goodall returned to England to begin classes at Cambridge University. When she showed her method of research to her professor, Robert Hinde, he said that animals were not given names in a study. They were given numbers. Also, he felt her style of writing sounded more like a novel than a scientific report. Animals could not think or have emotions like humans.

What Goodall had done was introduce a completely new approach to animal study.

When I first got to Cambridge in 1961, I had no undergraduate degree. I had not been to college, and there was [sic] many things about animal behavior that I did not know. I had not been taught that it was wrong to give names to my study subjects—it would have been more scientific to give them numbers. . . . For one thing, I did not think of the chimps as "study subjects" but as individuals, each with his or her own personality. I was learning *from* them, not only *about* them. On a more practical level, I would never have been able to remember who was who if they only had numbers.[1]

In the meantime, word of mouth was spreading about this unknown "Miss Goodall" who was conducting scientific research. She received two invitations to speak at scientific conferences. The first, titled "Primates," was held in London in the spring of 1962. She was the only field researcher at the conference, and the only one without a college degree. Her presentation revealed fascinating new discoveries from a study no one even knew was going on.

People had a difficult time believing Goodall. She was an unknown without any scientific credentials, and she was challenging the very definition of man. At her second conference, one scientist dismissed her entirely. Who would believe a woman who was young, blonde, and did not have a scientific background?

Back to Gombe

With the semester finished, Goodall arrived back at Gombe on July 8, 1962. To her great relief, the chimps remembered her. She quickly returned to work.

One day after returning to camp, her assistants told her that an adult chimp had strolled into camp and stayed for an hour feeding on the nuts of an oil palm tree next to Goodall's tent. A similar report came in the following day.

The next day she stayed at camp to see if the chimp would return. "I recognized him at once from having seen him in the forest."[5] In fact, it was the same chimp Goodall had seen eating meat, *and* the same one she had seen fishing for termites. It was David Greybeard.

He continued to visit the camp to feed on the nuts. Soon, he started to eat bananas that Goodall left out for him.

> [One day] he actually took a banana from my hand. . . . He stood up and hit the trunk of a tree, rocking slightly from foot to foot. But when he took the fruit there was no snatching—he was amazingly gently from the first.
>
> After that I began carrying a couple of bananas with me up in the mountains, and when I met David he would come up and take them, sitting close beside me, to the astonishment of his companions who gazed wide-eyed at the behavior of their fellow ape.[6]

It was only a short time before Goliath and William came to camp to get their hands on the bananas as well.

Thanks to the Bananas a Successful Article

When the National Geographic Society began to fund Goodall's study, it was agreed that she would write an article for their magazine. Unfortunately, her photographs were not up to the magazine's standards. The magazine would not publish the story if the photographs were not good. They hired a professional photographer, Hugo van Lawick, to go to Gombe with Goodall.

The chimpanzees allowed Lawick to get great photographs and video, thanks to the banana-feeding system. In August 1963, *National Geographic* published its first article by Goodall, titled "My Life With Chimpanzees."

A Complex Species

Goodall told a vivid story of her life living with wild chimpanzees. She introduced some of the chimpanzees she had come to know: David Grey-beard, Goliath, William, the F Family, Huxley, Count Dracula, and Mr. McGregor.

The article described the species' social structure. Chimpanzees have their own language made of calls and gestures. Sometimes one throws a tiff over something or a fight breaks out, but these are generally rare and last only a few minutes. By and large, the species is affectionate and loving.

"Mutual grooming plays an important part in the social life of chimpanzees, and two friends, or even a small group, will sit quietly for hours searching through each others' long black hair for specks of dirt, grass seeds, or ticks."[7]

Goodall's writing described an intimate scene between a female chimp, Mrs. Maggs, and her daughter, Jo. After waking from a nap together, Jo "climbed to a branch above the nest and hung down, kicking and twisting. . . . Her mother reached up and patted her, pushing her to and fro, until Jo, delighted, tumbled down on top of her. Mrs. Maggs, her legs in the air, bounced Jo up and down with her feet and then suddenly bent her knees so that Jo collapsed in a heap of waving arms and legs."[8]

One time, Goliath waved an ax in anger when Goodall refused to give him more bananas. She described how the heavy downfalls brought on a spectacular show she called a "rain dance." Meat eating and toolmaking sightings were also included.

The article was a huge success. Although some questioned Goodall's judgment for putting herself at such risk in the African wild, most praised her courage. Months before, Goodall had written in her journal: "My future is so ridiculous. . . . I just squat here, chimp-like, on my rocks, pulling out prickles & thorns, and laugh to think of this

⬆ Jane Goodall and Hugo Van Lawick, her husband, are visited by
a curious monkey while setting up their photographic equipment
at the Gombe Reserve.

unknown 'Miss Goodall' who is said to be doing scientific research somewhere."[9]

Now, Jane Goodall was an international celebrity and inspiration to many, and she was also in love. On March 28, 1964, Jane Goodall and Hugo van Lawick married in London.

Goodall's Ambitious Proposal

A few weeks before Goodall and Lawick married, they met with President Melvin Bell Grosvenor of the National Geographic Society. They discussed future plans at Gombe, a second article, a television special, and a book deal with publisher Houghton Mifflin.

Goodall predicted that it would take at least ten years of close observation and recording to get a full understanding of chimpanzee behavior and society. A permanent research center was needed. The National Geographic Society said they would have to think about it.

Leakey believed that Goodall's plans were premature. He thought she should complete her Ph.D., free up some time, and hire more help with the research. Goodall thought otherwise. She continued to send plans to Leakey, even drawings of the buildings she had in mind. Leakey, who always supported Goodall's work, soon put her vision into action.

New Additions to the F Family

"Flo amekwisha kuzaa," read the letter from the cook, Dominic, who looked after the camp while Goodall was away. "Flo has had her baby."

The news came just before the wedding. The bride and groom cut their honeymoon short and hurried back to Gombe. Baby Flint was already seven weeks old when the newlyweds returned to camp. Goodall could now document the development of an infant chimpanzee in the wild.

Even more exciting was what happened when Lawick held out a banana to the mother. Flo "[c]uddling her baby between belly and thigh, . . . came toward us on three limbs, followed by Fifi and jaunty Figan . . . [and] calmly took a banana. . . . The moment was unforgettable; we were filled with amazement that a wild chimpanzee mother trusted us enough to bring her baby close to us."[10]

Goodall could now observe more closely the intimate dynamic of a chimpanzee family. Since Flo was not afraid of Lawick, the photographer could record the F Family on camera.

A New Campsite Goes Up

Goodall and Lawick decided to move their campsite a little farther away from the beach where the fisherman cast their nets. Reports had come in that some chimpanzees had raided the huts of African fisherman. They were concerned that the locals could get hurt, since the chimpanzees had lost their fear of humans. Also, at camp the chimpanzees were going into tents, chewing clothes and chairs, and digging up wires that had been placed underground.

One day, while Goodall was at the new camp, she got a radio call from Lawick. She could not make out what he was saying. Suddenly, "[u]p over the top of the hill came my husband, running as never before, carrying a wooden box and shouting something about bananas. Close behind him bounded 14 chimpanzees, all with their hair on end and screaming with excitement."[11] Goodall quickly threw bananas all around the ground and got out of the way. While the chimps feasted in delight, Lawick said, "It was my one horror that the chimps would catch up and find out that the box was really empty!"[12]

The strategy worked. A banana-feeding station was set up at the new camp, and the chimpanzees stayed.

The Staff Grows Bigger

When Goodall's first study was published in *National Geographic* magazine in 1963, she was flooded with letters from all over the world. People praised her work and congratulated her fearlessness. For many readers, she had become an inspiration.

One writer's enthusiasm paid off. Edna Koning, a twenty-four-year-old from Holland, expressed her life-long ambition to work with animals. She begged to be Goodall's secretary in the chimp research. The help could definitely be used, and Edna joined the team. She arrived at Gombe in April 1964.

Goodall realized that she needed to organize her research so in her absence, Edna could replace her in data collecting. A daily record book was created to keep track of individual chimp sightings, fights and outbursts, feeding sites, illnesses and injuries, interactions with baboons, and more.

The workload was getting too large for the staff of three. It was necessary to hire an assistant to help manage the record books. In October, a young English woman named Sonia Ivey joined the team. There were now forty-five chimpanzees visiting the camp.

More Tools and Meat

Goodall and her husband were in the forest one day watching some chimps. Lawick noticed one named Evered pick up a handful of leaves and put them in his mouth. "Look!" said Hugo. "Whatever is he doing?"[13] Evered then took the leaves out of his mouth. The leaves were in a crumpled mass.

"Holding them between first and second fingers, he dipped them into a little hollow in the trunk beside him," Goodall recorded. "As he lifted out the mashed greenery, we saw the gleam of water. Our eyes opened wide as we watched Evered suck the liquid from the leaves!"[14]

As he could not reach the water in the trunk, he had made another tool, a "sponge," to soak up the water to drink. Goodall and Lawick made an artificial water bowl in one of the fallen tree trunks back at the new camp. More chimps did the same as Evered had, crumpling the leaves in their mouths and using them as sponges to gather the water. The behavior showed intelligence and problem-solving skills.

Goodall also reported more meat eating. When she witnessed David Greybeard eat meat in 1960, it was the meat of a bushpig. Four years later, it came as a great surprise when she saw a chimp eating the flesh of a baboon.

The Social Hierarchy Changes

Within a chimp community, there is a male hierarchy, with one male as the alpha, or leader. "When we left the reserve at the [end of 1963] before the wedding, Mike [a male chimpanzee] was cowed and nervous, flinching at every movement and sound." Mike was always getting attacked and threatened by the rest of the adult males, even

○ Chimp drumming on oil can.

though he was as big as they were. "On our return
we found a different Mike. He was feared by every
individual in the community. We shall never be
sure, but it seems likely that by leaving empty
kerosene cans lying about, we ourselves had
helped his rise to power."[15]

Chimpanzees, when they are excited or frustrated, put on what are known as charging
displays. They break into a run, throwing rocks
and sticks, dragging big branches, leaping through
the trees, stamping around and smacking the
ground. At the new camp, the chimpanzees
started using tables and chairs and other objects in
their displays. Mike found a way to use them to

his advantage. He started to bang empty kerosene cans together to imitate loud charging sounds. This scared off the other males, since chimpanzees do not like loud noises except for those they make themselves. This clever move cleared a path for him to the top of the group.

Communication

After Mike's rise to power, the other chimpanzees showed their respect by hurrying to him, "bowing or reaching out toward him. Mike may touch them briefly with his hand, or he may simply sit and stare."[16]

Goodall came to understand communication between chimps. In fact, they communicate in a variety of ways that are similar to humans. They use handshakes, pats on the back, tickling, punching, and kicking. When frightened or nervous, a chimp will grab onto another chimp. Physical contact is important to the species, especially mutual grooming.

When greeting one another, chimpanzees sometimes kiss or embrace. "Goliath was sitting when David came plodding along the path. Catching sight of each other, the two friends ran together and stood upright face to face, all their hair on end. . . . [T]hey swaggered slightly from foot to foot before flinging their arms around each other with small screams of pleasure and excitement."[17]

A Permanent Research Center

The camp now had a new makeover. Goodall's proposal for a permanent research center had been approved by the National Geographic Society in November 1964. Although not all of what Goodall envisioned would be realized, she was pleased with the three aluminum buildings that were constructed. The largest building had a room for working and storing files, two smaller bedrooms for Edna and Sonia, a tiny kitchen, and a storage area. The second building was where Goodall and Lawick slept. The third, and smallest, building served as a banana storehouse.

This research center provided a permanent place for graduate students and other scientists to study chimpanzees.

Time for a Break

Goodall's research was growing and she was spending many more hours in the field. She still had her Ph.D. thesis to finish, a few important lectures to give in the coming months, her book to think about, and a chapter to complete titled "Mother-Offspring Relationships in Free-ranging Chimpanzees" for a book collection called *Primate*

Ethology. She was in the midst of writing a second piece for *National Geographic,* too.

In August, she was treated for exhaustion. Her doctor advised at least six weeks of rest.

In March 1965, Goodall returned to Cambridge to finish her Ph.D. thesis, and Lawick went off on another assignment for *National Geographic*. Their two assistants remained at Gombe to continue research.

More Discoveries Revealed to the World

The success of the banana-feeding station at the new camp produced some major scientific data at Gombe. Goodall described it all in "New Discoveries Among Africa's Chimpanzees." It was her second article written for *National Geographic* magazine, published in the December 1965 issue. At the end of that month, CBS aired the television special, *Miss Goodall and the Wild Chimpanzees.*

She was also now Dr. Jane Goodall, having successfully completed her Ph.D. at Cambridge.

Epidemic

It was November 1966 when the staff at Gombe started to notice the change in a number of chimpanzees. Four-year-old Gilka had a paralyzed wrist. Both Faben and Madam Bee's one arm were paralyzed, too. Olly could barely walk on one of

⬆ Jane Goodall, her husband Baron Hugo Van Lawick and their son, "Grub," together on the shores of Lake Tanganyika where the Jane Goodall special, *The Baboons of Gombe,* was filmed.

her feet. David Greybeard had lost much use of one of his legs. The sight was terrible.

They had been infected with polio from the people of a nearby village. Polio is a disease that can cause temporary or permanent paralysis. Immediately, vaccines were ordered and given to all the staff at Gombe. Since the human disease had been passed to the chimpanzees, they could pass it back to humans. The vaccine was also placed in the bananas that were fed to the chimps.

By January of the following year, the epidemic was finally over. Four chimpanzees had died and five had partial paralysis.

Two years later, a flu epidemic struck Gombe and took the life of chimpanzee David Greybeard.

Of all the species in the world, chimpanzees are most closely related to humans. They can catch many known human infectious diseases.

Being a Mother

On March 4, 1967, the Goodall-Lawick family introduced a new addition to their family. Hugo Eric Louis van Lawick was born. His nickname was Grub.

Jane Goodall had been watching Flo raise her children for nearly three years now. "I had learned from Flo that distraction rather than punishment was the best way to teach a small infant. But I had also learned the importance of discipline and consistency. In the end I raised my own son on a mixture of wisdom gleaned from Vanne, Flo, . . . and mother nature."[18]

Dr. Goodall loved being a mother. She cut down the amount of time she spent at Gombe to devote more time to her son. Students had come to study the wild chimpanzees. And someone was hired as senior scientist of Gombe to supervise the students.

To raise money for the Gombe Research Center, Goodall wrote articles and attended conferences to promote the ongoing program. She also began to lecture in the United States. Her first book, *My Friends the Wild Chimpanzees*, was published by the National Geographic Society.

5

Busier Than Ever

When Louis Leakey sent Jane Goodall to study the behavior of wild chimpanzees at Gombe, he warned her that it might take ten years. A decade later, she knew there was so much still to learn about these intelligent and remarkable beings.

The research center was doing very well at the start of 1970. A permanent Tanzanian field staff had been created by recruiting individuals from villages around the park. Students were coming from around the world to assist in the field research. Specialized researchers arrived to gather information not only on chimpanzees but on baboons, other monkeys, birds, fish, snakes, and vegetation.

Fund-Raising

Since the conception of Jane Goodall's Gombe study in 1960, Louis Leakey was in charge of getting the funding. Beginning in 1971, all fund-raising responsibility was handed over to Dr. Goodall.

Funding for the field research at Gombe had been provided mainly by the National Geographic Society. This was changing. The costs to run the expanding facility at the reserve were increasing rapidly. The amount of money the National Geographic Society gave in support was lessening. This put Dr. Goodall in a difficult situation. How was she going to pay for research supplies and food to feed her staff? Where was she going to get the needed money?

Dr. David A. Hamburg worked at Stanford University's Department of Psychiatry. Leakey had introduced him to Goodall back in 1960. Dr. Hamburg had had a dream of his own—to build a seminatural chimpanzee laboratory on the California campus. When Jane explained the funding situation to Dr. Hamburg, he put forward a proposal that would put money into Gombe. Why not connect Stanford with Gombe? The research center could serve as a long-term field station for Stanford students.

The Grant Foundation agreed to provide funding Dr. Hamburg's plan and Gombe's budget for the next year. Soon after, Dr. Goodall and Dr. Hamburg joined forces with Dar es Salaam University, in Dar es Salaam, Tanzania's largest city. Dr. Goodall began teaching classes there in 1973. She was also a visiting professor of Psychiatry and Human Biology at Stanford from 1971 to 1975.

In 1971, her second book, *In the Shadow of Man,* was published. Goodall recounted her adventures and scientific discoveries at Gombe. It became an instant international success. It was written in a style that was entertaining, intelligent, and inspiring. The work would ultimately be translated into forty-seven different languages.[1]

Great Losses

The F family was the first wild chimp family Goodall followed and kept long-term records on. By 1972, Flo, who was then the mother of five children, was old and sick. When she passed away that year, it broke her son Flint's heart. He was eight years old at the time, and as Goodall wrote: "was still sleeping with her at night. . . . Flint immediately became lethargic and depressed. He scarcely ate, and seldom interacted with another chimpanzee. In this state he fell sick."[2]

Three weeks after his mother's death, Flint died. Goodall, now a mother herself, witnessed just how strongly death is able to affect the bond between a mother and her child.

Another great loss occurred that year. Louis Leakey, the British archaeologist and paleontologist, died on October 1, 1972.

A Secret Love

Derek Bryceson had just been made director of Tanzania's National Parks when he and Goodall were introduced in 1973.

Though he was much older than Jane Goodall, they got along very well. Mutual feelings for one another grew quickly, and the two started to have a secret love affair. The situation was dangerous for Goodall because she was still married to Hugo, and they shared a son, Grub.

Plane Crash Ties the Knot

Bryceson owned a small airplane and sometimes Goodall and Grub joined him on plane rides. One day, on a short plane ride to Ruaha National Park in Tanzania, a small plume of smoke appeared under the control panel. Nothing seemed wrong with the plane. The gauges were fine, there was enough fuel, and the engine light was not on.

When the plane finally landed, a herd of zebras was on the landing strip. The pilot lost control of the plane and it crashed into the ground.

The pilot shouted for everyone to get out of the plane before it blew up. Goodall quickly helped Grub out of the plane, but Bryceson was stuck. His door would not open and he could not move because luggage had been thrown about during the crash. Bryceson managed to dislodge himself and get out safely. Bryceson broke some ribs, but everyone else was unhurt.

This near-death experience connected Goodall and Bryceson even more. Goodall divorced Hugo in 1974. A year later, Bryceson and Goodall became husband and wife.

War and Kidnapping

Gombe Stream National Park was a peaceful place. Tanzania's neighboring African country, Zaire, however, was fighting a civil war.

On May 19, 1975, a boatload of forty armed men crossed Lake Tanganyika in the night and kidnapped four research assistants from the center at Gombe. The event made international headlines. The kidnappers demanded that a ransom of $460,000 be paid, two of their rebels be freed from jails in Tanzania, and a pamphlet be published internationally.[3] It took months of talks before the hostages were returned.

As the country of Zaire was still very unstable, there was concern that more kidnappings might happen. Stanford University ordered all its students to leave Gombe. Much of Goodall staff was now gone, too. Goodall moved to Dar es Salaam and was escorted to the reserve whenever she visited. Gombe had a strong and capable Tanzanian team to take over operations. Slowly, things returned to normal.

War and Cannibalism

"Recent years have brought an increased public awareness of the horrors of human aggressive behavior and a growing fear of what a terrible fate

☝ Candice Bergen and Jane Goodall watching chimps at Gombe in 1974.

this aggression may bring to the world. This concern in human society had led to an upsurge of interest in the aggressive behavior of nonhuman animals."[4]

Goodall wrote this sometime after the May 19 kidnapping. During the time of the kidnapping, she and her staff were recording another act of aggression—the gradual extermination of one group of animals by another, stronger, group. It would become known as the four-year war—the first recorded long-term act of warfare among nonhumans.

It began in 1970. The main Gombe study community began to split. Two separate chimpanzee communities formed. The Kasakela group claimed the park's land to the north, and the Kahama group stayed in the southern part. In 1974, five members of the Kasakela group brutally attacked a male from the Kahama group. Systematically, the Kasakela group killed members of the Kahama group over a four-year period.

This had a lasting impact on Goodall. Being an eyewitness to the brutal aggression that the Kasakela group displayed forever changed how she viewed these creatures. "I had known aggression could flare up, sometimes for seemingly trivial reasons; chimpanzees are volatile by nature, yet for the most part aggression within the community is more bluster and threat than fierce fighting—a whole lot of 'sound and fury signifying nothing.' Then suddenly we found that chimpanzees could be brutal—that they, like us, had a dark side to their nature."[5]

Goodall was living in Dar es Salaam when disturbing news reached her. "Passion has killed and eaten Gilka's baby."[6] She already knew from the four-year war that chimpanzees were ruthless enough to kill their own. This was the first time she heard that one was actually eating its own.

It happened again twice the following year. This time, Passion's daughter, Pom, committed the crimes.

One day, Goodall watched Pom climb up a palm tree. Passion stayed on the ground staring up. Another chimpanzee, Little Bee, was in the palm tree. She cradled her newborn chimpanzee in her arms.

Pom reached her hand out toward the baby. Little Bee started to scream and move away. Goodall picked up a stick and poked at Passion. Passion shooed the stick. Then she was racing up the tree. "Helpless [Goodall] shouted and threw things, but the second tree was tall, and already screaming and fighting had erupted high above."[7] Fortunately, Little Bee was able to escape.

Goodall and her team continued to follow the chimpanzee Passion and her family. Over a period of four years, the mother and daughter killed ten newborns. In 1978, Pom gave birth to a son and the killings stopped. Goodall was stumped as to the reasons for this cannibalistic behavior.

Yet, it was behavior not unknown to humans. It is believed by many experts that Neanderthals, whose origins date back more than three hundred thousand years, participated in cannibalism.

Of Major Significance

"Life and Death at Gombe" appeared on the front cover of *National Geographic* magazine in May 1979. In it, Goodall described the four-year war, Flo's death, and the crimes of Passion and Pom. She concluded the article by stating that "It is sobering that our new awareness of chimpanzee

Little Bee

violence compels us to acknowledge that these ape cousins of ours are even *more* similar to humans than we thought before."[8]

Goodall's observations of the Gombe chimpanzees engaging in warfare sparked a discussion about the aggressive behavior of humans. Just as humans was supposed to be the only toolmaker, humans were supposedly the only ones that participated in warfare.

With four years worth of notes and video, Goodall and her staff painted a picture that was hard to dispute. The Kasakela group did not just kill members of another community for the sake of it. They had a plan in mind—to wipe out the Kahama group. They preplanned and organized their moves. Crude weapons were used. The techniques employed by the Gombe chimpanzees in their fighting were all too similar to those used in human warfare.

This opened up a huge debate about the roots of aggression. One side believed that aggression was a natural part of us. The other side believed that aggression was a behavior we learned as a result of the environment around us.

For Jane Goodall, the dark and evil side of human nature was deeply rooted in humans' ancient past. "We had strong predispositions to act aggressively in certain kinds of contexts; and they were the same contexts—jealousy, competition for

food or sex or territory, fear, revenge, and so on—
that triggered aggression in chimpanzees."[9]

The Birth of the Jane Goodall Institute

When the Gombe student kidnapping hit international headlines, an emergency fund was created
to raise funds for the exorbitant ransom. Jane
Goodall thought the donations had paid the ransom amount, but that was not the case. She was
personally billed for $25,000.

She did not have the money. Most of the funds
she raised or made went to supporting the
research at Gombe. Most of the money made from
her book *In the Shadow of Man* went to a trust
fund for Grub that she could not touch.

One evening in 1977, friends visited Goodall
at Stanford University in California. What about a
tax-exempt charitable foundation, they suggested.
And so began the Jane Goodall Institute for
Wildlife Research, Education and Conservation.
The mission "is to advance the power of individuals to take informed and compassionate action to
improve the environment for all living things."

A group of board members was chosen and
volunteers signed up. At first, there was no office
and everything was done from each person's
home. Then, in the early 1980s, the offices moved
temporarily to San Francisco before settling into

its permanent space in Arlington, Virginia, outside of Washington, D.C.

The Process of Death

In September 1979, Goodall began a painful year-long watch of her husband, Derek, go through that process of dying. He had been diagnosed with cancer after experiencing severe stomach pains. He passed away on October 11, 1980.

After Bryceson's death, Goodall continued to run the Gombe Research Center. Again, money became an enormous issue. The annual budget to maintain operations was $33,000 dollars. Financial support from the Grant Foundation and National Geographic Society had decreased. The money she received from giving lectures would not cover the overhead. The Jane Goodall Institute was still in it primary stages and did not have the money. When her house was broken into and important supplies for Gombe were stolen, it seemed she had reached a dead end.

Gordon Getty, who became president of the Jane Goodall Institute in 1979, came through for his friend. He gave so generously that the institute was able to operate for several years. There was also enough money in the budget to do something about a serious issue Goodall had been concerned with for some years.

ChimpanZoo

In 1984, Jane Goodall turned fifty years old. She had made extraordinary discoveries about wild chimpanzees lives, and she had become one of the leading primatologists in the field.

That year, National Geographic released *Among the Wild Chimpanzees.* It is a documentary that shows the work of Goodall since her arrival at Gombe Stream National Reserve in 1960. In it, she talks about her work.

She had many thousands of pages of detailed records on chimpanzee life. The records described the intimate bond between mother and child, sibling rivalry, male dominance, friendship, and sexual appetites. She lectured and wrote about their ingenuity, their ability to reason and problem solve, and to make plans for the immediate future. She demonstrated how the curiosity of the chimpanzees resulted in imitation and practice that passed on patterns of behavior and expression from one to another.

Goodall began the preparations for her next project: ChimpanZoo. It was a research program that focused on studying chimpanzees in zoos and other places were they were held in captivity. The goal had three parts: The first part was to raise public understanding about chimp behavior. The second part worked to improve the lives of captive chimpanzees. The third part strove to join universities with zoos "to learn more about chimpanzees and their psychological and behavioral responses to a captive environment."[10] These investigations would then be compared with those from Gombe.

Although the budget proposal came to less than $20,000, it was turned down as too costly. It was too important to Goodall, so she paid the first year out of her own pocket.

In the beginning of 1986, she wrote to a friend about ChimpanZoo: "I must tell you that it is working, despite what everyone thought, most fabulously. . . . I think it's 13 zoos involved already. . . . So far it has cost nothing above Ann's salary and expenses because, as originally planned by me, the various zoos themselves provide us with on the spot funding. Or the local colleges."[11]

A 673-Page Masterpiece

It is difficult to imagine where Jane Goodall ever found the time for all of her projects and programs, article writing, lectures and conferences, university teaching, and child raising.

Her book *The Chimpanzees of Gombe: Patterns of Behavior*, almost seven hundred pages long, had been in the making since before her husband died. It was actually a monograph, a detailed written study on a specific subject. It started with an introduction

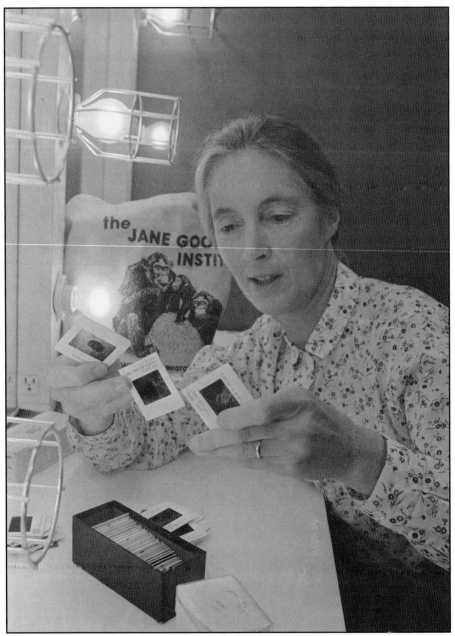

Jane Goodall goes through slides before making a presentation in Chicago on Saturday, May 9, 1982.

of all the chimpanzees she had met throughout her twenty-six years at Gombe. Then it delved into chapters dedicated to communication, relationships, dominance hierarchies, ranging patterns, feeding, hunting, aggressive group territoriality, sexual relationships, and skill with tools.

When it debuted in November 1986, it received excellent reviews. John H. Crook, reviewer for *The New York Times,* wrote:

> Miss Goodall's book may well emerge as the most significant ethological monograph based on field study in this half century. . . . [T]he similarity is so strong that philosophers may rightly concern themselves with what rights an animal as bright as some children should be accorded in a world where habitat destruction may soon mean that the chimpanzee no longer survives in the wild. One approach to such an issue might be to ask the animals themselves—as Dr. John Doolittle would most certainly have done. . . . Perhaps we human adults now need to use more imagination in our converse with these extraordinary "people."[12]

Turning Focus to Saving Lives

Shortly after *The Chimpanzees of Gombe: Patterns of Behavior* debuted, a conference titled "Understanding Chimpanzees" was held in Chicago, Illinois. People from all over the world attended the three-day event.

Goodall heard disturbing reports about the international trade of live animals. Baby chimps were being snatched from their families throughout the forests of Africa and sold illegally to biomedical research companies for research. So many baby chimps were being taken that the number of chimps available to maintain the species was falling quickly.

Goodall and about thirty other experts formed the Committee for Conservation and Care of Chimpanzees (CCCC). The mission of the CCCC is to improve the survival and living conditions of all chimpanzees. The CCCC wanted chimpanzee protection rights written into the U.S. law. They went to the National Institutes of Health (NIH), a U.S. federal agency that conducts and supports medical research and funds most of the animal research in the United States. Goodall persuaded the NIH to pass an amendment that prohibited the NIH from funding any project that involved the capture of chimpanzees from the wild.

Breaking Barriers

Two days after Christmas in 1986, Goodall watched a video titled "Breaking Barriers" given to her by the animal-rights group, People for the Ethical Treatment of Animals (PETA).

"We all sat watching the tape, and we were all shattered."[13]

The video had been secretly shot inside Sema, Inc., a biomedical research laboratory in Maryland. It showed the horrific living conditions of the primates inside the lab. The animals were caged in small chambers. One beat violently against the side of its cage. Another was dead in its cage. Goodall made copies of the video and sent them out to everyone she knew. She also signed a formal statement that was released to the public confirming the terrible living conditions of the primates at Sema laboratories.

John Landon, president of Sema, Inc., defended his company's treatment of animals in medical research. He invited Goodall to tour the labs instead of basing her accusations on a video.

On May 17, 1987, "A Plea for the Chimps," written by Goodall, was published in *The New York Times Magazine*. It was about the inhumane treatment of animals in medical testing and research. She then vividly described what she saw inside Sema, Inc. laboratories. The chimps' eyes were "dull and blank, like the eyes of people who have lost all hope, like the eyes of children you see in Africa, refugees, who have lost their parents and their homes."[14]

Goodall had huge issues with the fact that chimpanzees were being used at all in medical research, but she did not focus on that in her

Jane Goodall, who at this time operated four captive chimp sanctuaries in Africa, was considering building one in the United States to retire chimps used in medical research. She is shown here in an undated file photo from the 1980s.

essay. Instead, she focused on the inhumane way they were treated in medical labs.

Dr. Goodall, the CCCC, the Humane Society of the United States, and the Jane Goodall Institute organized a conference for the end of the year. The goal was to get the Animal Welfare Act amended to include a section that required special treatment for chimpanzees in laboratories and other captive situations. The act was scheduled to be finalized at the beginning of 1988.

Goodall spent the rest of 1987 tirelessly campaigning for the amendment change. She visited medical labs across the United States, spoke with senators and state representatives, hooked up with animal-rights lobbyist groups, and gave lectures across the country.

It was a huge disappointment when the finalized Animal Welfare Act did not include any of the changes Goodall fought to get in.

On a positive note, however, was that Goodall was invited back to Sema, Inc. laboratories.

CEO John Landon wanted to show her the changes he had made to the chimpanzees' living quarters. The tiny cages had been replaced by spacious ones that had play and sleeping areas. Lab workers also came in to play with the chimps.[15]

6

Through a Window

In 1987, as Jane Goodall was beginning her fifth book, she received a telegram. Pneumonia had killed nine chimps of Gombe, leaving two little orphans. One orphan, Mel, had lost his mother and wandered around completely lost. Spindle, who was not related to Mel and who had also lost his mother, took the orphan under his wing. For whatever reason, Spindle shared his food with Mel, let Mel sleep in his nest at night, and protected Mel. It was the first time this kind of behavior was observed among wild chimpanzees.

The book was taking a long time to complete because Goodall was working on other projects as well.

In the fall of 1990, *Through a Window: My Thirty Years With the Chimpanzees of Gombe* hit bookshelves. The book was the sequel to *In the Shadow of Man*. It reemphasized just how much chimpanzees are like humans. It talked about how the species was in danger because of such things as habitat loss and the sale of chimpanzees to companies for biomedical testing. It made a powerful statement about how important it was to fight for the species' conservation.

That year, *Chimps, So Like Us,* a documentary that takes place in Gombe Stream Chimpanzee Reserve, was nominated for an Academy Award. Narrated by Goodall, it guides the viewer through the reserve and shows the remarkable similarities between humans and chimpanzees. The second half of the film shows what is going on in biomedical laboratories and zoos. It talks about the cruel treatment that is being inflicted on the chimpanzees.

Saving the Orphans

The number of wild chimpanzees in the African country of Burundi had been declining. Much of the land the chimps inhabited was being cleared for farming, and the chimpanzees were being pushed out of their natural habitat. Goodall went to Burundi to talk with the president. The Jane Goodall Institute was able to convince the Burundi government to start a chimpanzee research project at the national park where most of the chimpanzees had moved.

The situation in Burundi was not only a result of deforestation. There was also the bushmeat business. Wild chimp meat is known as bushmeat, and natives in the area enjoy the taste of it. Many adult chimps in Burundi were killed for their meat. If its mother was killed, a young chimp would be left with no one to raise it. Goodall spoke with the president of the country and proposed that a sanctuary, a place of safety, be built for the orphaned chimpanzees.

While Goodall continued to fight for a safe and protected home for the orphaned chimps in Burundi, she also traveled to other parts of Africa. She was sent photos of chimpanzees living in a zoo in the People's Republic of Congo in Africa. The chimpanzees were in tiny cages made of concrete and iron bars. They were extremely malnourished and were not properly cared for by the zoo's staff.

Goodall met with the president of the People's Republic of Congo. She recommended that a sanctuary be made for all the orphaned and displaced chimpanzees. She explained that this idea would be good for the country. It would create jobs and encourage tourism. The project would also be good for education. Students could visit the sanctuary and learn about chimpanzees and other animals, too. And, of course, building the sanctuary would help the environment because the forest would be protected from the oil and logging companies.

These projects in Burundi and the People's Republic of Congo were ambitious and expensive. They would not happen overnight.

Going Back to Her Childhood

In February 1991, Gombe's thirtieth anniversary was held in Dar es Salaam, where Dr. Goodall was living. It was a five-day event.

During that week, Goodall visited many schools and gave presentations. She felt it was important that young people learn about wild chimpanzee conservation and how important it is to take care of the environment. After a presentation, Goodall would ask students to write down their names if they were interested in learning more.

Some days later, sixteen of those teens went to Goodall's house. They discussed some of the topics she had spoken about at their schools. The teens decided to begin a club dedicated to taking action to make the world a better place for people, animals, and the environment. Thus began the small beginnings of Roots & Shoots.

Goodall explained the meaning of the club's name and its message symbolically to a Roots and Shoots group in Toronto, Canada.

> "Symbolically, roots makes the firm foundation of the tree planting itself into the earth. Shoots of the tree can break through the brick walls as they move towards the sun. We see the brick walls as all of the things we have inflicted on the planet. The message is hope for hundreds of thousands of young people around the world who can break through these brick walls and make this world a better place."[1]

Goodall's aim for the club was "to raise awareness of African children about animals and thus plant the seeds for future conservation."[2] She took a minor role in the club's development and let the young people be in charge. Within four years, the club expanded to more than 250 Roots & Shoots groups all over the world. Twenty other countries were involved, including the United States.

Building Sanctuaries

About one hundred years ago, there were approximately two million chimpanzees living in the wild. The number had decreased to at most two hundred thousand. A number of factors contributed to the decline: Habitat destruction, population increase, hunting, commercial trade, and roads made by logging companies.[3]

The Texas-based oil company, Conoco, was looking for oil in the People's Republic of Congo when Goodall proposed to the country's president that a chimp sanctuary be built. Conoco agreed to fund the project, which cost $660,000.[4]

By the end of 1992, the sixty-five-acre Tchimpounga Sanctuary was ready for the orphaned chimps to move into. The Jane Goodall Institute ran the sanctuary. Unfortunately, it turned out to be very expensive to maintain. In the middle of 1993, Goodall received word that the Jane Goodall Institute had just about enough money to keep the organization running for only four more months.[5]

Goodall not only held a very successful fundraiser in Hollywood, but also donated fifty thousand dollars of her own money to keep the institute afloat.[6]

By the end of 1993, there was enough money to run the sanctuaries The Congo sanctuary was doing very well. In Bujumbura, Burundi, Goodall had set up a "halfway house" for ten orphans. Two other sanctuaries, one in Uganda, the other at Sweetwaters Game Reserve in Kenya, were built.

In Burundi, Goodall's plans fell through because of civil unrest. Fortunately, she was able to move the chimps to the Sweetwaters Game Reserve in Kenya.

Some people, however, questioned how Goodall was handling her conservation fight. and the money spent on sanctuaries. Why not use the money to preserve forests where chimpanzees still roam free?

Geza Teleki, who managed all of Goodall's programs in Africa, said to Goodall, "There are thousands of orphan chimps in Africa. How are you going to save them? We should worry about habitat, not orphans."[7]

Goodall saw it very differently. First came the individual. She believed that the chimp habitat needed to be protected. "But there are not that many people who after meeting an orphaned infant and looking into those desperate eyes, can turn away."[8]

Lake Tanganyika Catchment Reforestation and Education (TACARE)

In 1994, Goodall was flying over Gombe Stream National Park. The land in all directions outside the park was completely bare. All of the trees had been cut down. All of the areas natural resources were nearly gone. "How can we even try to conserve these amazing chimpanzees . . . if these people are struggling to survive?"[9]

If something was not done to replenish the area's natural resources, then soon Gombe Stream National Park would be gone, too. The villages would not survive without help, forcing the people living there to move somewhere else.

That realization soon developed into the program Lake Tanganyika Catchment Reforestation and Education (TACARE). This program primarily focused on growing trees and fruits and vegetables in thirty villages around the park. With time,

⊙ Orphaned by poachers, young chimpanzees are raised by volunteers and researchers at the Tchimpounga Sanctuary (part of JGI) in the Congo.

the program developed to include other projects: scholarships for girls to go to secondary school, improving the education of women and children, educating about safe sex and HIV/AIDS, and providing health care.[10]

A Reason for Hope

By the late 1990s, Goodall, who was in her sixties, spent more time in the air than on land. Her calendar was filled with visits to zoos and sanctuaries, media interviews, lectures, and business meetings around the world.

Jane Goodall's book *Reason for Hope* came out in 1999. It was unlike her other books. It was a memoir, a story about her life.

She reflected upon her childhood and the impact world events had on her. From an early age she knew about the effects of war. She saw photos of Nazi concentration camps during the Holocaust. She experienced the disappearance of her father and the death of her uncle in the war. These experiences had a long-lasting effect on Goodall's perception of the world.

Goodall wrote about her time at Gombe. As she spent more time in the forests of Tanzania with the wild chimpanzees, her view of the world and people's place in it changed. She realized that human beings were not the only creatures with minds and thoughts and feelings. She found that animals were much closer to humans than had always been thought.

To see the outside world as such a ruthless place was difficult for Goodall to understand. To see so much aggression and war perplexed her. To see humans so wasteful and destructive toward nature worried her. To see people treat animals so inhumanly tore her apart. Yet, in spite of all this, she still saw hope in a brighter future for the world. She believed that the world could change for the better. At the end of her memoir, Goodall laid out her four reasons for hope.

Her first reason for hope was the very intelligent and creative human brain. It has the capacity to do amazing things, including improve the world in which we live.

Her second reason for hope was the determination of young people. Young people possess amazing creative energy and passion. It is important that they become informed about all that is happening around the world. Young people are the world's future. The more informed and empowered they are at a young age, the more they will see that they can truly make a difference.

Goodall's third reason for hope is the resilience of nature. She often gives the example of Nagasaki, a city in southwest Japan that was wiped out by an atomic bomb at the end of World

War II. Scientists said that nothing would be able to grow for at least thirty years. Yet, soon after, small plants began to sprout, and, amazingly, a small tree survived the blast. The strength of nature against human destruction gives her hope for the future.

Her fourth reason for hope was the indomitable human spirit. Here she is talking about individuals who are courageous and committed. They do not let anyone or anything stop them from achieving their dreams. These amazing individuals inspire and become symbols of hope.

She wrote:

"It is easy to be overwhelmed by feelings of hopelessness as we look around the world. . . . There is the terrible pollution around the world, the balance of nature is disturbed, and we are destroying our beautiful planet. There are fears of new epidemics for which there will be no drugs, and, rather than fight the cause, we torture millions of animals in the name of medical progress. But in spite of all this I do have hope."[11]

A New Millennium

On April 12, 2000, Jane Goodall's mother, Vanne, passed away. That year also marked the fortieth anniversary of their arrival at Gombe.

On July 14, 2000, Jane Goodall made a visit to Tanzania to celebrate her forty years at Gombe. Only two others from the beginning were still around. One was a staff worker who was just a boy when Jane and her mother arrived. The other was Fifi, Flo's daughter. When Goodall first came to Gombe, Fifi was only a baby.

Goodall also went back to Gombe to raise more money. The Jane Goodall Institute had grown into a global organization. It not only funded the continuing research at Gombe but also Roots & Shoots, TACARE, the many sanctuaries in Africa, and other projects. Five million dollars a year is needed to sustain all the programs.

A Decorated Woman

Dr. Jane Goodall has worked tirelessly in her fight to help not only chimpanzees but also humans, wildlife, and the environment. She places great focus on young people. The Roots & Shoots program supports projects led by young people in nearly one hundred countries.

On April 16, 2002, Dr. Goodall was asked by Secretary-General Kofi Annan of the United Nations (UN) to serve as a United Nations Messenger of Peace. "The United Nations Messengers of Peace are distinguished individuals . . . who have agreed to help focus worldwide attention on the work of the United Nations. . . . [T]hese prominent

Jane Goodall observes chimps in the Gombe Stream Reserve in 1961.

personalities volunteer their time, talent and passion to raise awareness of United Nations' efforts to improve the lives of billions of people everywhere."

Ban Ki-moon became the new UN secretary-general in 2007. He reappointed Dr. Goodall as a United Nations Messenger of Peace.

Goodall also created the Chimpanzee Guardian Project, halfway homes for injured and orphaned chimps found in the wild. She has won numerous honors and awards for her work.

Everyone Can Help

Kids have the power to get involved in saving the earth and animals. Learn the issues that threaten the health of our world. Read about endangered species. Visit a nearby zoo. Ask questions.

It is important that people work to save earth's species and the environment. The earth is a complex living organism that cannot survive unless everything is balanced. Unfortunately, human beings are offsetting this balance as the world population grows and global warming harms the environment.

Since the beginning of Jane Goodall's study of chimpanzees, she has worked tirelessly to protect the chimpanzees and their habitat, to educate people about species conservation, and to advocate for animal rights. Her work has extended also to include fighting for the environment and humans as well.

Goodall took on an assignment driven by a childhood dream. Today, she is still with that assignment, living a childhood dream that has led us to rethink ourselves, our closest relative, and the natural world in which we live.

Timeline

1934—April 3, Valerie Jane Goodall is born to Mortimer and Margaret Myfanwe Joseph Goodall in London, England.

1957—Visits Africa for the first time; meets Dr. Louis Leakey.

1960—Arrives with mother at Gombe Stream Chimpanzee Reserve in Tanganyika Territory (Tanzania) to study chimpanzees.

1962—Begins Ph.D. classes at Cambridge University, Cambridge, England.

1963—*National Geographic* magazine publishes first article "My Life With Chimpanzees."

1964—Marries Hugo van Lawick in London. National Geographic Society grants funds for permanent research center at Gombe Stream Chimpanzee Reserve.

1965—*National Geographic* magazine publishes second article "New Discoveries Among African Chimpanzees"; CBS airs TV special *Miss Goodall and the Wild Chimpanzees;* Completes Ph.D. at Cambridge University; now Dr. Jane Goodall .

1967—Son Hugo Eric Louis van Lawick is born; nicknamed Grub; First book, *My Friends the Wild Chimpanzees,* is published by National Geographic Society.

1971 —1975—Visiting professor of psychiatry and human biology at Stanford University.

1971—Second book, *In the Shadow of Man,* published.

1974—Divorces husband Hugo van Lawick.

1975—Marries Derek Bryceson.

1977—Starts Jane Goodall Institute for Wildlife Research, Education and Conservation.

1979—*National Geographic* magazine publishes third article "Life and Death at Gombe."

1980—Husband Derek Bryceson dies.

1984—National Geographic Society releases documentary *Among the Wild Chimpanzees;* ChimpanZoo is established to study chimpanzees in captive environments.

1986—*The Chimpanzees of Gombe: Patterns of Behavior* monograph is published.

1987—Article " A Plea for the Chimps" appears in *The New York Times Magazine.* Campaigns for changes in federal Animal Welfare Act to include chimpanzees.

1988—*My Life with the Chimpanzees* published.

1990—*Through a Window: My Thirty Years with the Chimpanzees of Gombe* is published. Documentary *Chimps, So Like Us,* narrated by Goodall, is nominated for Academy Award.

1991—Goodall and 16 Tanzanian students found Roots & Shoots, the Jane Goodall Institute's global environmental and humanitarian education program for youth.

1994—Helps develop Lake Tanganyika Catchment Reforestation Education (TACARE) organization

1999—A memoir, *Reason for Hope* is published

2002—Accepts request to be a United Nations Messenger of Peace.

2003—Made a Dame of the British Empire.

2004—Awarded Nierenberg Prize for Science in the Public Interest.

2004—Presented with Honorary doctorate degree in science from Syracuse University.

2005—Presented with Discovery and Imagination Stage Award

2006—Receives the 60th Anniversary Medal of UNESCO (United Nations Educational, Scientific and Cultural Organization).

2007—Receives honorary doctorate degree in commemoration of Linnaeus from Uppsala University, Sweden.

2008—Receives honorary doctorate degree from University of Toronto.

2009—Named 2009 Year of the Gorilla patron.

Glossary

alpha—One that is socially dominant in a group of animals.

anthropomorphic—Giving nonhuman things human characteristics.

biomedical—Relating to biological , medical, and physical science.

bonobo—A separated species of chimpanzee, sometime called the pygmy chimpanzee.

bushmeat—The meat of wild animals that is sold illegally.

bushpig—A wild hairy pig found in forests and scrubland of sub-Saharan Africa.

charging display—A threatening action by a male chimpanzee.

curator—One in charge of a zoo, museum, or another place of exhibit.

deforestation—The process of clearing forests.

dominance—In the animal world, an individual or group with power over one another.

ethology—The scientific study of animal behavior under natural conditions.

habitat—The place where an animal or a plant normally lives.

herpetology—A branch of science that deals with amphibians and reptiles.

hierarchy—The ranking of group members based on ability or other skills.

ichthyology—A branch of science that deals with fish.

malnourished—Not fed enough; underfed.

paleontologist—A scientist who deals with eras in the past based on fossils.

predisposition—To be susceptible or responsive to something.

primates—A group of mammals that includes humans, greater apes (chimpanzees, bonobos, and orangutans), lesser apes (gibbons and siamangs), baboons, monkeys, and animals such as lemurs and marmosets.

primatologist—A scientist who studies primates, such as apes.

species—A group of organisms so similar to one another that they can interbreed.

zoologist—A scientist who studies animal life.

Chapter Notes

Chapter 1. The Rain Dance of the Chimpanzees

1. Dale Peterson, *Jane Goodall: The Woman Who Redefined Man* (Boston: Houghton Mifflin Company, 2006), pp. 235, 236.

Chapter 2. A Curious Child

1. Jane Goodall, *In the Shadow of Man* (Boston: Mariner Books, 2000), p. 3.

2. Dale Peterson, *Jane Goodall: The Woman Who Redefined Man* (Boston: Houghton Mifflin Company, 2006), p. 14.

3. Jane Goodall, *Reason for Hope* (New York: Warner Books, 1999), p. 5.

4. Peterson, *Jane Goodall: The Woman Who Redefined Man,* pp. 22–23.

5. "Message From Africa," Page by Page Books, 2004. <http://www.pagebypagebooks.com/Hugh_Lofting/The_Story_of_Doctor_Dolittle/Puddleby_p1.html> (April 24, 2009).

6. Ibid.

7. Karin Davies, "Working for Animal Rights—Renowned Researcher Goodall Advocates Chimpanzee Havens," *The Seatle Times,* December 14, 1997. <community.seattletimes.nwsource.com/archive/?date=19971214&slug=257805> (April 24, 2009).

8. Goodall, *Reason for Hope,* pp. 12–13.

9. "An Encouraging Mother," Jane Goodall-Childhood, The Jane Goodall Institute n.d. <http://www.janegoodall.org/jane/childhood.asp> (April 24, 2009).

10. Goodall, *Reason for Hope,* p. 14.

Chapter 3. Off to Africa

1. Dale Peterson, *Jane Goodall: The Woman Who Redefined Man* (Boston: Houghton Mifflin Company, 2006), p. 101.

2. Jane Goodall, *Reason for Hope* (New York: Warner Books, 1999), p. 44.

3. Ibid., p. 55.

4. Jane Goodall, *In the Shadow of Man* (Boston: Mariner Books, 2000), p. 6.

5. "Jane Goodall—Early Years in Africa: Olduvai Gorge," The Jane Goodall Institute, n.d. <http://www.janegoodall.org/jane/early.asp> (April 24, 2009).

6. Goodall, *In the Shadow of Man* pp. 19–20.

7. Peterson, p. 189.

8. Goodall, *Reason for Hope,* p. 64.

9. Goodall, *In the Shadow of Man,* pp. 26, 28.

10. Goodall, *Reason for Hope,* p. 74.

11. Ibid.

12. Virginia Morell, "Jane Goodall, The Discover Interview," *DISCOVER Magazine*, vol. 28, no. 3, March 2007. <discovermagazine.com/2007/mar/the-discover-interview-jane-goodall> (April 24, 2009).

13. Ibid.

Chapter 4. First Important Discovery

1. Jane Goodall, "My Life Among Wild Chimpanzees," *National Geographic,* August 1963, <encarta.msn.com/sidebar_761593559/my_life_among_wild_chimpanzees.html> (April 24, 2009).

2. Learning From the Chimpanzees: A Message Humans Can Understand, *Science,* December 18, 1988: Vol. 282, no. 5397, pp. 2184–2185 <http://www.sciencemag.org/cgi/content/full/282/5397/2184> (April 24, 2009).

3. Virginia Morell, "Jane Goodall, The Discover Interview," DISCOVER Magazine, vol. 28, no. 3, March 2007. <discovermagazine.com/2007/mar/the-discover-interview-jane-goodall> (April 24, 2009).

4. Dale Peterson, *Jane Goodall: The Woman Who Redefined Man* (Boston: Houghton Mifflin Company, 2006), p. 276.

5. Goodall, "My Life Among Wild Chimpanzees," p. 294.

6. Ibid.

7. Ibid., p. 289.

8. Ibid., p. 287.

9. Virginia Morell, "Jane Goodall, The Discover Interview", DISCOVER Magazine, vol. 28, no. 3, March 2007. <discovermagazine.com/2007/mar/the-discover-interview-jane-goodall> (April 24, 2009).

10. Jane Goodall, "New Discoveries Among Africa's Chimpanzees," *National Geographic*, vol.128, no. 6, December 1965, p. 804.

11. Ibid., p. 806.

12. Ibid., p. 808.

13. Ibid., p. 813.

14. Ibid.

15. Ibid., p. 812.

16. Ibid., pp. 812–813.

17. Ibid., p. 825.

18. Jane Goodall, *Reason for Hope* (New York: Warner Books, 1999), p. 89.

Chapter 5. Busier Than Ever

1. Dale Peterson, *Jane Goodall: The Woman Who Redefined Man* (Boston: Houghton Mifflin Company, 2006), p. 482.

2. Jane Goodall, "Life and Death at Gombe," *National Geographic*, vol. 155, no. 5, May 1979, p. 614.

3. Peterson, p. 559.

4. Goodall, "Life and Death at Gombe," p. 598.

5. Douglas Cruickshank, "A Conversation With Jane Goodall," Salon.com, October 27, 1999. <http://www.salon.com/people/feature/1999/10/27/goodallint/index.html> (April 24, 2009).

6. Goodall, "Life and Death at Gombe," p. 616.

7. Ibid., p. 619.

8. Ibid., p. 620.

9. Jane Goodall, *Reason for Hope* (New York: Warner Books, 1999) p. 134.

10. Dr. Virginia Landau, "ChimpanZoo History," ChimpanZoo, The Jane Goodall Institute, n.d. <http://www.chimpanzoo.org/history.html> (April 24, 2009).

11. Peterson, p. 591.

12. John H. Crook, "An Undaunted 'Starer at Animals'," *The New York Times,* August 24, 1986. <www.nytimes.com/1986/08/24/books/an-undaunted-starer-at-animals.html?&pagewanted=all> (April 24, 2009).

13. Peter Miller, "Jane Goodall," *National Geographic,* vol. 188, no. 6, December 1995, p. 126.

14. Ibid.

15. Ibid., p. 127.

Chapter 6. Through a Window

1. "Roots and Shoots: Shaping Tomorrow's Conservationists," *Green Living.* n.d. <www.greenlivingonline.com/article/roots-shoots-shaping-tomorrows-conservationists> (April 24, 2009)

2. Peter Miller, "Jane Goodall," *National Geographic,* vol. 188, no. 6, December 1995, p. 126.

3. "Eco-Tourism in Africa," *Big Picture TV*, September 1, 2002. <http://www.bigpicture.tv/videos/watch/f7177163c>(April 24, 2009).

4. Dale Peterson, *Jane Goodall: The Woman Who Redefined Man* (Boston: Houghton Mifflin Company, 2006), p. 635.

5. Miller, p. 120.

6. Peterson, p. 635.

7. Miller, p. 117.

8. Ibid., pp. 117, 120.

9. "The TACARE Project," Big Picture TV, September 1, 2002. <http://www.bigpicture.tv/videos/watch/6c8349cc7> (April 24, 2009)

10. Virginia Morell. "Jane Goodall, The Discover Interview," *DISCOVER Magazine*, vol. 28, no. 3, March 2007. <discovermagazine.com/2007/mar/the-discover-interview-jane-goodall> (April 24, 2009).

11. "Jane Goodall—My Four Reasons for Hope," *The Jane Goodall Institute*, n.d. <http://www.janegoodall. org/jane/essay.asp> (April 24, 2009).

Further Reading

Bardhan, Sudipta. *Up Close: Jane Goodall.* New York: Penguin Group, 2008.

Greene, Meg. *Jane Goodall: A Biography.* Amherst, N.Y.: Prometheus Books, 2008.

Haugen, Brenda. *Jane Goodall: Legendary Primatologist.* Minneapolis, Minn.: Compass Point Books, 2006.

Stefoff, Rebecca. *Chimpanzees.* New York: Benchmark Books, 2004.

Internet Addresses

Jane Goodall Institute
http://www.janegoodall.org/

Hanging Out With Chimps (National Geographic Explorer)
http://magma.nationalgeographic.com/ngexplorer/0209/articles/mainarticle.html

Creative Feature: Chimpanzees (National Geographic Kids)
http://kids.nationalgeographic.com/Animals/CreatureFeature/Chimpanzee

Index